Nov. 2014

This book belongs to:

Love,
Nonna + Papa

MonumentCity Editions
Diffusion - distribution:

contact@parischeri.net
www.parischeri-shop.com

Illustration and text by: Cécilia Sagouis

Translated from the French by Dominique Krayenbühl

Printed in Belgium
First edition: 2009
Second edition: 2012
ISBN: 978-2-918211-03-7

Paris Parade

MonumentCity Editions

Cécilia Sagouis

Paris Parade

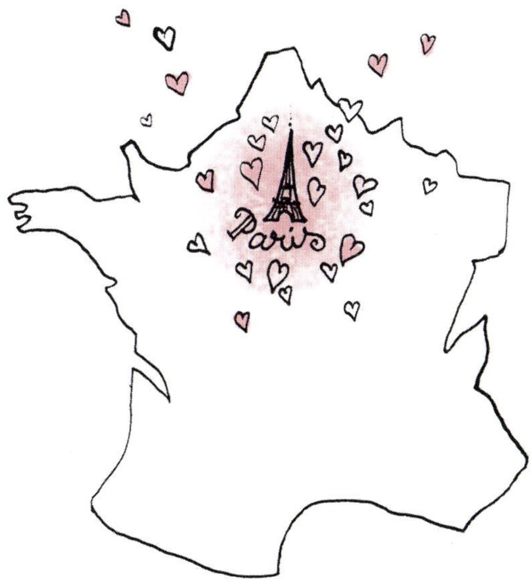

For this visit to Paris

put  in your 

and  in your 

and let's go!

But Paris is nothing without its Parisians...

Let's go towards the center of Paris, the Île de la Cité, and admire the jewel that is the cathedral of Notre-Dame de Paris.

A gargoyle has been standing guard...
...for over 800 years!

A bit further flower market stretches out at the foot of the Palais de Justice, or Conciergerie, where Marie-Antoinette was locked up during the Revolution...

...and on the Quai de la Mégisserie...

...the bird market.

The bouquinistes have their little shops set up on the quays... small green shells which open for the bargain hunters delight.

Here, on the quays, summer vacationers enjoy the deckchairs of Paris-Plage...

...those who feel the cold take the Bateaux-Mouches.

On the other side of the Boulevard de Sébastopol soars the Centre Pompidou, a museum of modern and contemporary art.

Here is a young man
who savours his
jambon-beurre, his ham
and butter sandwich...

...under the attentive eyes of
these other famous Parisians,
the gentlemen pigeons.

This tender giant is a sculpture by Henri de Miller,
at the foot of Saint-Eustache church.

Let's cross the Pont de la Tournelle.
The statue of Sainte Geneviève
watches over the Parisians.

Left bank... the Quartier Latin.

A waiter wipes his glasses behind the bar,
called zinc.

Let's go for a stroll in the streets:

A yellow diamond shape with a red feather...
it's a newsagent.

A green cross...
it's a pharmacy.

The grocery is still open... for the benefit of night owls.

The Panthéon offers its imposing architecture to the Great Men that rest in its crypt.

But where is this nanny going to?
She is taking her children
for a walk...

...in the Jardin du Luxembourg.

Oh! a statue?

No! A mime artist!

Here is the Hôtel des Invalides where the tomb of Napoleon the First is located.

Close by, The Thinker meditates in the garden of the Musée Rodin.

Let's return to the right bank...

A pyramid in the middle of a Renaissance palace?
It's the Louvre.
It houses exceptional works: antiquities from all continents and a collection of paintings. Here is the most famous one:

The Mona Lisa
or La Gioconda by
Leonardo da Vinci.

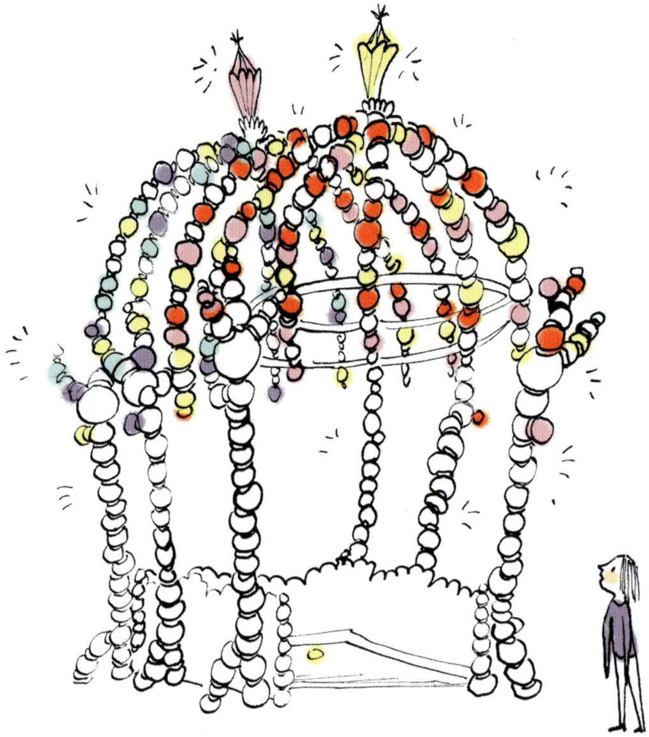

A cage of pearls... the metro station of Palais-Royal...
...competes with a bicycle station...

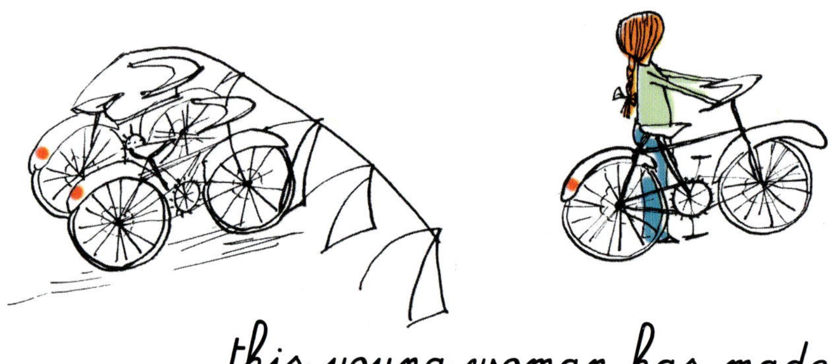

this young woman has made her choice...

...and heads for the Place de la Concorde,
the former Place de la Révolution.

In 1836, the oldest antique in Paris, an obelisk brought back from Egypt, was erected right in the middle!

The Champs-Elysées connects the Place de la Concorde
to the Arc de Triomphe.
This famous avenue was the cradle of haute couture.

One can take a leisurely stroll along its walks, in the shade of big plane trees.

Let's take the metro or metropolitan...

...a musician enlivens
our underground journey.

We find another haven of greenery,
the Parc Monceau, a garden that dates back to
the eighteenth century with its fake ruins.

Let's visit Paris Grands Boulevards...
La Madeleine, a church whose architecture is
reminiscent of a Greco-Roman temple.

Difficult to resist the gourmet shop windows which surround the square...

...and here is the sweet star of the moment: the macaron. They exist in all colors and all flavors!

Let's walk down the main boulevards, everywhere traces of the nineteenth century embellishments: here a Morris column...

...there a Wallace fountain.

The Place Vendôme is famous for its jewelers.
A man dominates the square from the top of a column.
It's a statue of Napoléon dressed as
Caesar.

For the 1st of May, streets pedlars sell May Bells, or muguet, those very pretty, small spring bells.

We can admire famous ballets at the Opéra Garnier...

...and taste the honey produced in the beehives placed on the opera's roofs.

What is this man in green doing?
He is cleaning the streets of Paris.

Let's slowly climb up
to the highest point in Paris, Montmartre!

On the Place du Tertre, painters display their creations to the tourists.

The Sacré-Cœur of Paris houses the
Savoyarde, one of the biggest bells in the world.

Vineyards, right in the middle of the capital!
About a hundred bottles of wine are produced each year.

And then there is a huge romantic parc, the Parc des Buttes-Chaumont, with its grottoes and its small belvedere or temple of the Sibyl.

But in Paris there is also a forest, in the Bois de Boulogne.

Here are some children in the Jardin d'Acclimatation, near the big aviary.

To reach it, take the little train...

There, puppet shows are staged.

At the other end of Paris, in the Bois de Vincennes, lies a pretty zoo.

Here it is, at last, the Eiffel Tower, symbol of Paris. Three hundred meters high! On a fine day, you can see as far as 70km all around.

All you have to do now is to go to Paris!

My trip to Paris

Date:

My impressions:

My favorite monument:

My favorite museum:

My favorite garden:

My favorite restaurant:

My favorite dish:

My favorite pastry:

What I didn't like at all!:

See you soon!